THE COOK'S COLLECTION
❋
TEMPTING
APPETISERS

Author: Annette Wolter
Photography: Susi and Pete Eising and Odette Teubner
Translated by UPS Translations, London
Edited by Josephine Bacon

CLB 4160
This edition published in 1995 by Grange Books
an imprint of Grange Books PLC, The Grange, Grange Yard, London SE1 3AG
This material published originally under the series title "Kochen Wie Noch Nie"
by Gräfe und Unzer Verlag GmbH, München
© 1995 Gräfe und Unzer Verlag GmbH, München
English translation copyright: © 1995 by CLB Publishing, Godalming, Surrey
Typeset by Image Setting, Brighton, E. Sussex
Printed and bound in Singapore
All rights reserved
ISBN 1-85627-765-8

THE COOK'S COLLECTION

❉

TEMPTING APPETISERS

Annette Wolter

Grange
BOOKS

Introduction

Whether you are entertaining friends with a lavish dinner party, or offering a simple starter to your family, an appetizer should simultaneously whet the appetite, taking the edge off any gnawing hunger, and prepare the tastebuds for the dishes to follow. Maybe because it comes first, or perhaps just because the servings are smaller and more tempting than main course portions, there are many people who gain more enjoyment from an appetizer than from the main dish. In short, it is worthwile taking particular care over the preparation of this important part of the meal.

An appetizer is generally light, the portion is relatively small, and the flavours are usually anything but bland. The taste should awaken the palate and prepare the diner for what is to come. It is important that the flavours in your first course complement those of the food that comes next. It is usually a good idea to select your main course first, then to choose a starter that will balance its flavours, ingredients and presentation. The same ingredients should not be featured in both the appetizer and main course dishes, but a theme should nevertheless be maintained.

Packed with inspirational new recipes, this delightful book is designed to make the job of planning a meal easier and more interesting. There is something here for everyone. So whether you are an experienced cook looking for ideas, or an eager beginner whose confidence needs bolstering, you will find this book of tremendous value when creating original and tasty appetizers for any occasion.

Each recipe serves four, unless otherwise indicated

Asparagus Tips au Gratin

1kg/2¼lbs asparagus
1tsp salt
1 sugar cube
4 slices white bread, each
weighing 50g/2oz
2 tbsps soft butter
200g/7oz cooked prawns
4 tbsps crème fraîche
4 tbsps freshly grated Jarlsberg
cheese
2 tbsps finely chopped dill

Preparation time:
15 minutes
Cooking time:
30 minutes
Nutritional value:
Analysis per serving, approx:
1490kJ/355kcal
23g protein
13g fat
37g carbohydrate

Preheat the oven to 220°C/
430°F/Gas Mark 7. If using
white asparagus, thinly peel it
from top to bottom, and cut
off the woody ends.• Bring the
salt and sugar to the boil in 2
l/3½ pints of water. Tie the
asparagus spears into three
bundles, and cook in a covered
saucepan for 10-15 minutes
depending on thickness of
stems.• Drain the asparagus and
cut about 6cm/2½in off the tips
(Reserve the rest of the stems
and the cooking water to make
soup.)• Spread the bread with
butter.• Rinse the prawns in
cold water and drain. Divide
the asparagus tips between the
slices of bread and arrange the
prawns on top.• Place the slices
of bread on a baking sheet
lined with aluminium foil.
Combine the crème fraîche
and the grated cheese, and
pour this over the prawns.•
Cook on the middle shelf of
the oven until the top is
golden brown.• Garnish with
dill.• A green salad is a good
accompaniment.

Our Tip: Salsify may be prepared
in the same way.

Roe on Dill Toast

50g/2oz softened butter
100ml/4fl oz quark or crème fraîche
Sea salt
2 tsps lemon juice
2 tbsps finely chopped dill
4 slices wholemeal bread
80g/3oz trout roe

Preparation time:
15 minutes
Nutritional value:
Analysis per serving, approx:
• 1130kJ/270kcal
• 4g protein
• 22g fat
• 13g carbohydrate

Beat the butter with the quark or crème fraîche and salt until creamy. Stir in the lemon juice and dill. • Toast the bread and spread it with the dill butter. Cut the slices in half diagonally and top with the roe.

Stuffed Watermelon Slices

½ watermelon
1 tsp pink peppercorns
100g/4oz shrimps
50g/2oz quark
100g/4oz crème fraîche
Sea salt
2 tsps lime juice
1 tsp honey
1 tbsp finely chopped dill
1 dill sprig

Preparation time:
15 minutes
Nutritional value:
Analysis per serving, approx:
• 795kJ/190kcal
• 8g protein
• 9g fat
• 17g carbohydrate

Cut the melon into four slices, and cut a shallow, semi-circular slice out of the flesh of each piece, leaving the green outer skin intact. • Crush the peppercorns in a

...ortar and mix with the
...rimps, quark, crème fraîche,
...asoning and dill. • Fill the
...ollow in each melon slice
...ith ¼ of the mixture and
...rnish with dill and shrimps.

9

Prawn Cocktail

16 king prawns
4 lettuce leaves
125ml/4fl oz mayonnaise
3-4 tbsps tomato ketchup
1-2 tbsps dry sherry
Juice of half a lemon
Pinch each of salt and sugar
½ tsp white pepper

Preparation time:
15 minutes
Nutritional value:
Analysis per slice, approx:
• 940kJ/225kcal
• 9g protein
• 17g fat
• 9g carbohydrate

Peel and de-vein the prawns. Rinse under cold running water and dry. • Wash the lettuce leaves; line four cocktail glasses with the dried leaves. • Make the sauce using the mayonnaise and the remaining ingredients. Pour into the lined glasses. Hang four prawns from the rim of each glass, to be dipped in the sauce.

Shrimp Cocktail

24 shrimps in their shells
100g/4oz mushrooms
Juice of 1 lemon
Pinch each of salt, white pepper
and sugar
3 tbsps mayonnaise
1 lettuce heart
100g/4oz freshly cooked
asparagus tips

Preparation time:
20 minutes
Nutritional value:
Analysis per serving, approx:
• 670kJ/170kcal
• 18g protein
• 8g fat
• 4g carbohydrate

Peel and de-vein the shrimps; rinse under cold running water and drain. • Clean the mushrooms and slice finely. Mix together the lemon juice, salt, pepper, sugar and mayonnaise. Break the lettuce into leaves, wash, dry and cut into strips. Mix the shrimps, asparagus tips, lettuce strips and mushrooms together with the sauce. • Serve in four cocktail glasses.

Lobster Cocktail

1 small frozen lobster
½ bunch dill
Juice of ½ lemon
3 tbsps mayonnaise
Salt and freshly ground white
pepper
Pinch of sugar
Few lettuce leaves of your
choice
4 dill sprigs
½ lemon

Thawing time:
2 hours
Preparation time:
0 minutes
Nutritional value:
Analysis per serving, approx:
630kJ/150kcal
4g protein
13g fat
3g carbohydrate

Remove the lobster from its packaging and thaw in a refrigerator. • Scoop out the flesh and cut it into thin slices. Wash, dry and chop the dill. • Mix together the lemon juice and mayonnaise; season with salt, pepper and sugar. • Stir the lobster meat into the sauce, then mix in the dill. • Wash and dry the lettuce; line a salad bowl with the leaves. Arrange the cocktail in the bowl. Decorate with washed dill sprigs, half slices of lemon and the lobster claws.

Maatjes Herrings with Mustard

1 onion, cut into rings
500ml/16fl oz water
125ml/4fl oz vinegar
2 tbsps sugar
4 juniper berries
8 maatjes herring fillets
weighing 50g/2oz each
1 untreated orange
125ml/4fl oz cream
1 shallot
2 tsps medium-hot prepared
mustard
1 tsp mustard powder

Preparation time:
40 minutes
Marinating time:
1 day
Nutritional value:
Analysis per serving, approx:
• 1820kJ/435kcal
• 18g protein
• 33g fat
• 17g carbohydrate

B oil the water with the vinegar, sugar, juniper berries and onions cut into rings, then allow it to stand and cool. • Cut the maatjes herring fillets into pieces, pour the marinade over them and store them, covered, in a cool place for 24 hours. • Drain off the marinade. Wash the orange and finely shred a small piece of the peel. Remove the rest of the peel and the pith. Slice the orange, then cut the slices into quarters. • Mix the pieces of herring with the onion rings and orange slices. Sprinkle with 1 tsp of shredded orange peel. • Whip the cream until stiff. Peel and finely grate the shallots. Combine the shallots and mustard with the cream. Serve the mustard sauce with the herring.

Canapés with Mackerel Cream

Makes 8 canapés:
1 smoked mackerel (about 300g/10oz)
250g/8oz quark
1 tbsp lemon juice
Pinch each of salt, freshly ground white pepper and paprika
4 slices of bread
1½oz/30g softened butter
black olives
15g/½oz fresh dill

Preparation time:
20 minutes
Nutritional value:
Analysis per serving, approx:
880kJ/210kcal
13g protein
15g fat
7g carbohydrate

Separate the mackerel flesh from skin and bones. Purée the fillets, and combine with the quark and lemon juice. Season the cream with salt, pepper and paprika. • Remove crusts from the bread and spread with butter. Cut each slice in half diagonally to produce eight triangles. • Take a piping bag with a large star-shaped nozzle and pipe the mackerel spread over the bread. Stone the olives and cut them into fine strips. Wash the dill and pat dry. Garnish the canapés with strips of olive and dill.

Our Tip: *The cream spread ingredients can be varied at will. It tastes marvellous if prepared with 300g/10oz of smoked salmon, for example. In this case, use whipped cream and quark in equal measure. A little lemon juice gives extra zing, and instead of olives, use paper-thin onion rings and strips of smoked salmon as a garnish.*

Spiny Lobster Tails with Melon

4 frozen spiny lobster tails,
200g/7oz each
4 tomatoes
2 shallots
1 onion
1 stick celery
1 fresh tarragon sprig
1 small honeydew melon
1 bay leaf
1 tbsp caraway seed
Salt
4 drops Tabasco sauce
2 egg yolks
2 tbsps prepared hot mustard
4 tbsps oil
4 tbsps cognac
125ml/4fl oz cream
1 small piece of tinned truffle
(optional)

Thawing time:
8 hours
Preparation time:
1 hour
Nutritional value:
Analysis per serving, approx:
• 1880kJ/450kcal
• 16g protein
• 24g fat
• 35g carbohydrate

Thaw the lobster tails in the refrigerator for about 8 hours. • Skin the tomatoes and slice them into eighths. Dice the onions and shallots. Wash the celery and tarragon; slice the celery and chop the tarragon finely. Cut the melon in half and remove the pips. Hollow out the flesh with a melon-baller and mix the flesh with the tomatoes, tarragon and shallots. Chill the mixture. • Boil the onion, celery, bay leaf, caraway, 1 tbsp salt and Tabasco sauce for 5 minutes in 1l/1¾ pints of water. Place the lobster tails in the pan and cook for 5 minutes over a low heat until tender; leave them in the liquid to cool. • Beat the egg yolks with the mustard and some salt. Mix in the oil drop by drop with half the cognac and a little truffle juice if using. Whip the cream until stiff and combine with the cognac liquid. • Arrange the salad in the melon halves. Cu

...e lobster tails in half
...ngthways. Scrape out the
...esh and arrange it in the
...ells, decorate with small
...ces of truffle and sprinkle
...ith the remaining cognac.
...rve with the mustard
...ayonnaise.

15

Stuffed Avocados

50g/2oz millet
½ tsp sea salt
4 tbsps milk
100g/4oz shelled peas
2 hard-boiled eggs
50g/2oz smoked salmon
2 fully ripe avocados
1 tbsp sunflower oil
1 tbsp each lemon juice and cream
2 pinches five-spice powder
Pinch of white pepper
1 tbsp each chopped chives and chopped parsley

Preparation time:
30 minutes
Nutritional value:
Analysis per serving, approx:

- 1695kJ/405kcal
- 11g protein
- 32g fat
- 17g carbohydrate

Boil the millet with the salt and 125ml/4fl oz water for 10 minutes in a covered pan. Add the milk and the peas and cook for 10 minutes until tender; strain through a sieve. Slice the eggs and cut the salmon into fine strips. Halve the avocados, remove the stone and hollow the fruit out a little more with a teaspoon. Mix the egg slices, salmon strips and avocado flesh with the remaining ingredients. Fill the avocado halves with the mixture.

Spring Cocktail

100g/4oz young spinach
1 shallot
200ml/4fl oz low-fat quark
200ml/4fl oz crème fraîche
150g/5½oz shrimps
2 tsps soya sauce

½tsp paprika
1½ tbsps chopped chives
1 bunch of radishes

Preparation time:
5 minutes
Nutritional value:
analysis per serving, approx:
1085kJ/260kcal
17g protein
18g fat
6g carbohydrate

Wash the spinach and separate the leaves and stalks; divide between four cocktail glasses. • Peel and finely chop the shallots, and mix with the quark, crème fraîche, shrimps, soy sauce, paprika and 1tbsp chives. Spoon the mixture onto the spinach; garnish with the radishes and the remaining chives.

Coley with Spinach

250g/8oz spinach
250g/8oz coley fillet
2 tbsps lemon juice
pinch of pepper
2 tbsps olive oil
2 hard-boiled eggs
1 tbsp soya sauce
1 tomato
1 slice bread
1 tbsp chopped chives

Preparation time:
5 minutes
Nutritional value:
analysis per serving, approx:
835kJ/200kcal
9g protein
10g fat
8g carbohydrate

Wash the spinach and chop coarsely. • Rinse the fish and season with 1 tbsp lemon juice and the pepper; cover and steam in the oil and 1 tablespoon of water for 5 minutes. Turn the fish, scatter with a sprinkling of spinach leaves and cook for a further 5 minutes. • Break up the fish. Slice the egg and reserve four slices. Stir the fish pieces, egg slices, soya sauce and remaining lemon juice into the spinach. • Garnish with the remaining egg, some small tomato wedges, toast and chives. Serve hot.

Herring Fillets with Spicy Mayonaise

4 maatjes herrings
100ml/4fl oz mayonnaise
100ml/4fl oz sour cream
1 bay leaf
6 grains allspice
Pinch each of salt, sugar and
freshly ground white pepper
2 onions
2 gherkins
2 sharp apples
1 bunch of dill
Some lettuce leaves

Preparation time:
50 minutes
Nutritional value:
Analysis per serving, approx:
• 2715kJ/650kcal
• 27g protein
• 52g fat
• 18g/¾oz carbohydrate

Slit the herrings along the belly and clean, taking care to remove the dark membrane. Make a cut in the skin on the back of the fish and pull off the skin, starting at the head. Remove both head and tail, and bone the fish. Soak the fillets in cold water for 30 minutes. • Meanwhile, mix the sour cream and mayonnaise and add the bay leaf and allspice; season with salt, pepper and sugar. Cut the onion into rings and finely dice the gherkins. Wash, quarter and core the apples, then slice them thinly. Stir the apples, onions and gherkins into the cream and mayonnaise mixture. Wash and dry the dill; reserve a few sprigs for the garnish, then chop the rest finely and stir into the sauce. Remove the bay leaf. • Remove the fillets from the water; dry them and arrange them on a plate. Partially coat the fillets with the sauce and garnish them with the dill, washed lettuce and lemon, apple or onion slices, if desir Serve the remaining sauce separately.

Fish Salad
with Mustard Sauce

500g/1lb 2oz haddock fillets
Juice ½ lemon
1 onion
1 bay leaf
250ml/9fl oz dry white wine
1½ tsps salt
250g/8oz tomatoes
½ bunch spring onions
125g/5oz button mushrooms
Some tarragon leaves
3 tbsps tarragon vinegar
1 tsp medium-hot mustard
1 tsp sweet mustard
4 tbsps oil
Freshly ground white pepper

Preparation time:
30 minutes
Nutritional value:
Analysis per serving, approx:
• 1010kJ/240kcal
• 25g protein
• 9g fat
• 8g carbohydrate

Rinse the fish fillets and sprinkle with a little lemon juice. Use a sharp knife to cut the fillets into slices. Remove any bones. Peel the onion and insert the bay leaf inside it. Dilute the white wine with 500ml/16fl oz of water, add the onion, a teaspoon of salt and bring to the boil. Put the fish strips into the water and cook over a gentle heat for between 3 and 5 minutes. Remove and allow to cool. • Peel the tomatoes, quarter and remove the seeds. Rinse and trim the spring onions and chop finely. Cut the mushrooms into thin slices. Rinse the tarragon and cut the leaves into thin strips. Mix the vinegar and both types of mustard in a bowl. Add the oil a little at a time, then the tarragon with the remaining salt and pepper. • Carefully mix the fish with the other ingredients and coat with the dressing.

20

Asparagus Salad with Smoked Salmon

1 kg/2¼lb white asparagus
500g/1lb 2oz green asparagus
1 tsp salt
2 sugar cubes
3 tbsps tarragon vinegar
4 tbsps sunflower oil
Salt and white pepper
Some dill leaves
200g/7oz crème fraîche
250g/8oz smoked salmon cut
into wafer-thin slices
2 hard-boiled eggs

Preparation time:
1 hour
Nutritional value:
Analysis per serving, approx:
• 2090kJ/500kcal
• 24g protein
• 37g fat
• 19g carbohydrate

Peel the asparagus from the tip to the base and trim off any wooden stalk. Make two bundles of white asparagus and one bundle of green. • Bring sufficient water to the boil, adding the salt and sugar cubes. Place the white asparagus in the boiling water, cover and cook for 10 minutes. Add the green asparagus and cook for a further 10 minutes. • Drain the asparagus and separate the bundles. Mix the vinegar with the oil, pepper and salt and pour over the asparagus. • Rinse the dill, shake dry, chop and stir into the crème fraîche. • Arrange the salmon slices alongside the asparagus. Peel the eggs, chop them finely and sprinkle over the asparagus. • Serve the dill sauce separately with toast.

Scallops au Gratin

4 fresh scallops
1 shallot
50g/2oz spinach
100g/4oz mushrooms
75g/3oz butter
125ml/4fl oz white wine
4 tbsps double cream
Salt
4 tbsps breadcrumbs
2 tbsps freshly grated cheese

Preparation time:
1 hour
Nutritional value:
Analysis per serving, approx:
• 2070kJ/495kcal
• 35g protein
• 29g fat
• 17g carbohydrate

Break open the scallop shells, remove the white flesh and the orange coral and rinse. Clean the shells and boil them for a few minutes. • Chop the shallots finely. Wash the spinach thoroughly, drain well and chop fincly. Clean and dry the mushrooms and slice thinly. • Heat 50g/2oz of the butter. Fry the mussel flesh and the coral briefly, remove from the pan and keep hot. Fry the chopped shallot in the butter until it becomes transparent. Add the spinach and mushrooms and heat for 5 minutes. • Add the wine and double cream and bring to the boil; season with salt. Return the mussel flesh and the coral to the pan and reheat for a short time. • Heat the oven to 220°C/450°F/Gas Mark 8. • Spoon the mixture into the scallop shells, mix the breadcrumbs with the cheese, and scatter this mixture over the scallop sauce. Cut the rest of the butter into small pieces and dot the mixture with it. • Bake the scallops on the top shelf of the oven for about 10 minutes or until a crisp golden crust has formed.

King Prawns in Garlic Butter

2 cloves garlic
Salt
1 bunch of parsley
125g/5oz softened butter
Freshly ground black pepper
½ tsp lemon juice
12 king prawns
1 small untreated lemon

Preparation time:
15 minutes
Cooking time:
15 minutes
Nutritional value:
Analysis per serving, approx:
  1695kJ/405kcal
  32g protein
  30g fat
  2g carbohydrate

Chop the garlic cloves coarsely, sprinkle with salt, then crush. Wash, dry and finely chop the parsley; reserve 1 tbsp of it. Mix the butter with the garlic, parsley, pepper and lemon juice. • Coat a flameproof dish with half the butter mixture. Heat the oven to 240°C/450°F/Gas Mark 8. • Wash the prawns thoroughly and remove the heads. Using a sharp knife, de-vein the prawns. Pat them dry them, arrange them in the dish and scatter the remaining parsley over them. • Bake the prawns on the middle shelf of the oven for 10–15 minutes or until they are crisp and red on the outside. • Wash, dry and slice the lemon. Serve the prawns garnished with the rest of the parsley and half slices of lemon. • Fresh, crisp French bread and a well-chilled white wine make a delicious accompaniment.

Turbans of Sole en Croûte

4 sheets of frozen puff pastry
(250g/8oz)
4 fillets sole
Bunch tarragon
Salt and freshly ground white
pepper
4 shallots
250g/8oz button mushrooms
125ml/4fl oz white wine
250ml/8fl oz single cream
Pinch cayenne
2 egg yolks
Juice 1 lemon
4 tbsps dry sherry
½ lemon
Sprigs of chervil

Thawing time:
30 minutes
Preparation time:
1 hour
Nutritional value:
Analysis per serving, approx:
• 1800kJ/430kcal
• 23g protein
• 27g fat
• 13g carbohydrate

Spread out the pastry slices and leave them to thaw at room temperature.• Halve the sole fillets lengthways, rinse in cold water and pat dry. Rinse the tarragon, shake dry and chop finely. Rub salt and pepper into the skin of the fish and sprinkle with tarragon. Roll up the fillets and secure with a cocktail stick. Heat the oven to 220°C/450°F/gas mark 7. • Peel the shallots and chop finely. Rinse and trim the mushrooms and cut into slices. • Using a sharp knife, cut a square inside the perimeter of the pastry slices about 1cm/½ inch from the edge, but cut only two-thirds of the way through the sheet. Rinse a baking tray under cold water. Place the pastry slices on the wet surface and bake on the middle shelf of the oven for 20 minutes or until golden brown. • Bring the white wine to the boil and add the shallots and mushrooms. Place the

rolled sole in the wine and simmer for 10 minutes over a medium heat. Remove the rolls and keep them warm. • Add the cream to the hot stock and season with cayenne and a little salt. Return to the boil and reduce the liquid by a half. Beat the egg yolks with the lemon juice. Remove the sauce from the heat, stir in the egg yolks and sherry, but do not re-heat. • Take the puff pastry squares from the oven and lift out the pastry 'lid'. Remove the cocktail sticks from the sole fillets and place two pieces in each pastry square. Pour the sauce over the fish and rest the 'lid' on top. • Rinse and dry the lemon and cut into thin slices. Rinse the chervil and pat dry. Arrange the pastries on a warmed dish and serve garnished with lemon slices and chervil. • Serve with sherry, preferably the same sherry that was used for the sauce.

Our tip: Instead of fillets of sole, try using eight scampi for the pastry squares. Prepare the sauce first and then cook the prawns slowly. Use ground ginger in place of cayenne.

25

Scampi au Gratin with Cucumber

16 Dublin Bay prawns
½ cucumber
2 egg yolks
2 tbsps white wine
Salt and freshly ground white pepper
Pinch of sugar
125g/5oz well chilled butter
1 bunch of fresh, or ½tsp dried, tarragon

Preparation Time:
30 minutes
Nutritional value:
Analysis per serving, approx:
• 1590kJ/380kcal
• 23g protein
• 30g fat
• 3g carbohydrate

Peel, de-vein, rinse and dry the prawns. Peel the cucumber and halve it lengthwise. Scoop out the seeds with a spoon, then cut it into slices. • Butter a flameproof dish and heat the oven to 250°C/450°F/Gas Mark 8. • Fill the dish with the prawns and cucumber. Whisk the egg yolks, wine, salt, pepper and sugar in a bowl standing in warm water, gradually whisking in the flaked butter. Wash the fresh tarragon, chop the leaves finely and stir into the sauce. Pour the sauce over the prawns and cucumber. Bake in the oven for 5 minutes. • A baguette crisped in the oven makes a delicious accompaniment.

Our Tip: Try slices of blanched courgette instead of the cucumber in this gratin.

Vol-au-vents with Shrimp Ragoût

125g/5oz mushrooms
2 tsps lemon juice
'0g/2oz butter
' tbsps flour
'25ml/4fl oz hot chicken stock
'25ml/4fl oz dry white wine
'50ml/8fl oz cream
'50g/8oz shrimps
'00g/7oz freshly cooked
sparagus tips
alt and freshly ground white
epper
'inch of sugar
' egg yolks
' bunch of dill
' vol-au-vent cases (frozen)

'reparation time:
') minutes
'utritional value:
'nalysis per serving, approx:
'1670kJ/400kcal
'14g protein
'31g fat
'10g carbohydrate

Wash and clean the mushrooms, pat them dry and slice thinly; sprinkle with lemon juice and fry in half the butter until the liquid has evaporated. • Prepare a sauce using the remaining butter, the flour, the chicken stock and the wine; allow it to boil for a minute, then add the cream. Add the shrimps, asparagus tips and mushrooms and simmer for a further 5 minutes. • Heat the oven to 200°C/400°F/Gas Mark 6. • Season the ragoût with salt, pepper and sugar. Mix the egg yolks with 2 tbsps of hot sauce. Thicken the ragoût with this mixture but do not allow further boiling. Wash and dry the dill, chop it finely and stir into the ragoût. • Heat the vol-au-vent cases briefly in the oven. Fill with the shrimp ragoût.

Asparagus Salad with Chervil

1kg/2¼lbs green asparagus
1 tsp salt
Pinch sugar
250g/8oz button mushrooms
250g/8oz prawns
Bunch chervil
1 shallot
300ml/12fl oz soured cream
1 tbsp lemon juice
Salt and freshly ground white pepper

Preparation time:
40 minutes
Nutritional value:
Analysis per serving, approx:
- 920kJ/220kcal
- 20g protein
- 9g fat
- 15g carbohydrate

Peel the asparagus working from the tip to the base. Cut off the woody stalks and tie the asparagus into four bundles with kitchen thread. • Boil sufficient water with the salt and sugar to cover the asparagus. Place the asparagus in the boiling water and cook for 20 minutes. • Remove and dry. Trim the mushrooms, rinse, drain and cut into thin slices. Rinse the prawns and dry. Peel the shallot and chop finely with the chervil. Reserve a few prawns for the garnish. Mix the shallots and chervil with the soured cream, lemon juice, salt, pepper, mushroom slices and the rest of the prawns. • Place the drained asparagus on a serving dish and pour over the chervil cream. Garnish with the prawns.

Mango with Chicken

‎ chicken breast fillets
‎ tsp curry powder
‎ tbsp sesame seeds
Pinch salt
50g/2oz butter
‎ very ripe mangoes
‎ small tomatoes
Salt and black pepper
‎ tbsps any favourite relish

Preparation time:
‎ hour

Nutritional value:
Analysis per serving, approx:
1680kJ/400kcal
28g protein
14g fat
41g carbohydrate

Rinse the chicken breast fillets and dry. Rub the curry powder, sesame seeds and salt into the flesh. Cover and leave to stand for a few minutes. • Melt the butter in a frying pan until foamy, reduce the heat to low and fry the chicken breasts for 3 minutes on each side. Leave the fillets to cool to room temperature. • Peel the mangoes and carefully cut the flesh into thin slices before removing the stone. Rinse the tomatoes, dry, halve and remove the seeds. Sprinkle salt and pepper inside the tomato halves and fill each one with a tablespoon of relish. • Cut the chicken breasts into thin slices and arrange them on a serving dish with the mango slices and tomatoes. • Sprinkle a little curry powder and toasted sesame seeds on top (optional).

Our tip: *Try slices of fresh pineapple fried in butter instead of mango. Leave out the tomatoes and top with lightly whipped cream and pink peppercorns.*

29

Prunes with Bacon

To make 20:
10 rashers thin-cut rindless
bacon (100g/4oz)
20 stoned prunes
1 tbsp oil

Preparation time:
20 minutes
Nutritional value:
Analysis per serving, approx:
• 295kJ/70kcal per portion
• 1g protein
• 5g fat
• 9g carbohydrate

Halve the bacon rashers and wrap them around the prunes, securing with a cocktail stick if necessary. • Heat the oil in a frying pan and fry the bacon over a medium heat until crisp. Drain and serve.

Dates with Mascarpone

To make 16:
16 fresh dates
1 tbsp pine kernels
100g/4oz Gorgonzola or other
blue cheese
100g/4oz Mascarpone
Freshly ground green pepper

Preparation time:
25 minutes
Nutritional value:
Analysis per serving, approx:
• 630kJ/150kcal per portion
• 3g protein
• 4g fat
• 10g carbohydrate

Rinse the dates, pat dry and cut open lengthways to remove the stones. • Fry the pine kernels without fat over a medium heat, stirring well. Cook until lightly browned, then remove and chop coarsely. • Place the Gorgonzola and the Mascarpone in a bowl and mix together with a spoon. Season the cheese mixture with green pepper and spoon it into a piping bag with a star nozzle. • Pipe the mixture into the open dates and sprinkle with the toasted pine kernels.

Pawpaw Morsels

1 ripe pawpaw
2 tsps lemon juice
50g/2oz wafer-thin slices
Parma ham
Coarsely ground black pepper
Some leaves of lemon balm

Preparation time:
15 minutes
Nutritional value:
Analysis per serving, approx:
• 335kJ/80kcal
• 3g protein
• 5g fat
  7g carbohydrate

Quarter the pawpaw and remove the seeds with a teaspoon. Use a sharp knife to peel the fruit, then cut each quarter into wedges and sprinkle with lemon juice. • Cut the slices of Parma ham into strips about 3cm/1 inch wide. Wrap the pawpaw slices in the ham and sprinkle a little pepper on top. • Arrange the wedges on a plate and garnish with rinsed lemon balm. Secure the ham to the pawpaw with cocktail sticks.

Exotic Slices

4 x 125g/5oz chicken breasts
Salt and freshly ground white
pepper
2 tbsps oil
3 tbsps mayonnaise (50% fat
content)
1 tsp curry powder
1 tsp lemon juice
Pinch sugar
1 chicory head
4 kiwi fruit
1 mango
2 tbsps desiccated coconut
8 slices thick-cut bread for
toasting
30g/1oz softened butter
8 leaves lemon balm

Preparation time:
30 minutes
Nutritional value:
Analysis per serving, approx:
• 2300kJ/550kcal
• 35g protein
• 25g fat
• 49g carbohydrate

Clean the chicken breasts. Pat them dry and rub in the salt and pepper. Brown in the oil and leave to cook over a gentle heat for about 10 minutes. • Leave the chicken to cool and then cut into slices. • Season the mayonnaise with the curry powder, lemon juice, salt and sugar. Trim the stalk from the chicory and cut the rest into rings. Rinse and leave to drain. Peel the kiwi fruit and mango. Cut the kiwi fruit into slices and the mango into thin wedges. Brown the coconut flakes in a frying pan without fat until golden brown, then set aside on a plate. • Toast the bread, leave it to cool and then spread with butter. Lay the chicory and chicken slices on the toast and then cover with the seasoned mayonnaise. Arrange the kiwi slices and mango on top and sprinkle with the toasted coconut flakes. Decorate with lemon balm leaves.

Salmon on Wholemeal

1 white radish
Salt and freshly ground white
pepper
1 tbsp chopped chives
125ml/5fl oz whipping cream
½ cucumber
4 slices wholemeal bread
30g/1oz softened butter
4 slices smoked salmon (about
200g/4oz)
2 sprigs dill leaves

Preparation time:
20 minutes
Nutritional value:
Analysis per serving, approx:
1300kJ/310kcal
10g protein
19g fat
22g carbohydrate

Peel the radish and grate
it coarsely. Add salt, pepper
and chopped chives and mix
together. Whip the cream until
stiff and add the radish
mixture. Peel the cucumber
and cut it into slices. • Butter

the bread thinly, arrange the
slices of cucumber over them,
then spread with the cream
and radish mixture. Finally fold
the salmon slices and lay them
loosely on top. Garnish with
the dill leaves. • Serve these
canapés immediately as the
radish and the cucumber slices
release water.

Our tip: *Use slices of raw ham
instead of smoked salmon. Cut
them into squares and arrange
them on top of the cream and
radish mixture. Sliced tomatoes
may be used instead of cucumber
slices.*

Minced Steak Terrine

To serve 10:
4 slices thick-cut white bread
200g/7oz cured pork slices
100g/4oz pickled gherkins
2 large onions
1 large green pepper
500g/1lb 2oz minced steak
4 eggs
1 tbsp hot mustard
1 tsp salt
Freshly ground black pepper
Pinch cayenne
Bunch chives
15g/½oz butter for greasing

Preparation time:
1 hour
Cooking time:
40 minutes
Cooling time:
3 hours
Nutritional value:
Analysis per serving, approx:
• 760kJ/180kcal
• 18g protein
• 10g fat
• 5g carbohydrate

Soak the bread in cold water. Finely chop the cured pork, gherkins and onions. Clean and trim the pepper and then cut it into cubes. • Place the minced steak in a bowl. Squeeze the water from the bread and combine with the minced steak and the other prepared ingredients. Add the eggs, mustard, salt, pepper and cayenne. • Heat the oven to 180°C/350°F/Gas Mark 4. Line the inside of a rectangular cake tin with greased non-stick baking paper. • Rinse and dry the chives. Snip the chives over the mixture, before kneading the 'dough' thoroughly. Carefully add it to the prepared tin and smooth over the surface. Cover the terrine with a double layer of baking paper, greased where the paper is in direct contact with the mixture, and place the tin in a large pan filled with boiling water. • Place it in middle of the oven and cook for 1 hour 40 minutes. Remove the baking paper 20 minutes before the end of cooking.

Beansprout Salad with Lamb

1 large onion
1 clove garlic
2 whole allspice
1 bay leaf
2 dried shiitake mushrooms
3 tbsps wine vinegar
1 tbsp vegetable stock granules
100g/4oz long-grain rice
300g/10oz leg of lamb
200g/7oz mushrooms
200g/7oz cucumber
1 red sweet pepper
200g/7oz beansprouts
2 tbsps sunflower oil
2 tbsps soya sauce
2 tbsps red wine vinegar
1 tsp mustard
1 tsp grated ginger
Generous pinch ground
cardamom
4 tbsps chopped chives

Preparation time:
30 minutes
Cooling time:
30 minutes
Nutritional value:
Analysis per serving, approx:
• 1505kJ/360kcal
• 20g protein
• 19g fat
• 24g carbohydrate

Peel the onion and attach the allspice, bay leaf and garlic clove with a cocktail stick. Place them in 500ml/16fl oz of water, bring to the boil, add the rice, the dried mushrooms, vinegar and vegetable stock granules and cook for 10 minutes. • Cook the meat with the rice for a further 30 minutes. • Rinse and trim the mushrooms, halving the larger ones. Peel the cucumber and dice. Add the mushrooms and cucumber to the meat and rice for the last 10 minutes of the cooking time. • Cut the red pepper into thin strips and blanch them in boiling water with the beansprouts for 3 minutes. Drain well. • Make a salad dressing from the remaining ingredients. • Drain the rice mixture in a colander but retain the water. Remove the spiked onion and garlic. Cut the meat and shiitake mushrooms into strips. • Mix all the ingredients with the salad dressing and a little of the retained liquid.

Bean and Sweetcorn Salad

150g/5½oz haricot beans
1l/1¾ pints water, boiled and
cooled
2 red onions
5 small tomatoes
100g/4oz cured pork slices
1 can of sweetcorn
(300g/10oz)
2 tbsps red wine vinegar
Salt and pepper
3 tbsps olive oil
1 hard-boiled egg
Some chervil or parsley leaves

Soaking time:
2 hours
Preparation time:
hours
Nutritional value:
Analysis per serving, approx:
1600kJ/380kcal
19g protein
16g fat
43g carbohydrate

Rinse the beans and soak overnight. • Cook the beans in the same water for about 1½hours. • Peel the onions and cut into thin rings. Rinse the tomatoes, drain and cut into slices. Cut the ham into strips and drain the sweetcorn. Drain the cooked beans and leave to cool. • Mix the vinegar with the salt, pepper and oil. Rinse the chervil or the parsley, shake dry and chop finely. • Mix the onion rings, tomato slices, sweetcorn and meat strips in with the beans. Pour in the vinegar dressing. • Garnish with the quartered hard-boiled egg and chopped chervil or parsley.

Roast Pork Cones filled with Apple and Horseradish

1 red pepper
1 green pepper
1 onion
Bunch chives
200g/7oz canned sweetcorn
3 tbsps white wine vinegar
2 tbsps olive oil
½ tsp salt
2 small apples
75g/3oz freshly grated
horseradish
125ml/4fl oz whipping cream
25g/1oz almonds
Salt
Pinch sugar
4 x 75g/3oz slices cold pork
Some lettuce leaves

Preparation time:
30 minutes
Nutritional value:
Analysis per serving, approx:
- 2100kJ/500kcal
- 18g protein
- 36g fat
- 29g carbohydrate

Cut the peppers in half lengthways and remove the pith, seeds and stalks. Rinse, dry and slice thinly.

Peel and chop the onion. Rinse and dry the chives and chop finely. Drain the sweetcorn and mix with the peppers, chopped onion and chives. Season with the vinegar, oil and salt. Cover and leave to stand for a few minutes. • Peel the apples and grate coarsely. Mix the grated apple with the horseradish. Whip the cream until thick. Chop the almonds finely and mix with the grated apple, horseradish, whipped cream, salt and sugar. • Spoon the mixture over the pork slices and roll up loosely. Serve with the sweetcorn and peppers on a bed of lettuce leaves.

Palm Hearts in Rolled Ham

1 onion
2 tbsps palm oil
1 tbsp curry powder
75g/3oz long-grain rice
125ml/4fl oz hot chicken stock
1 red pepper
1 banana
2 slices fresh pineapple
1 tbsp mango chutney
150ml/5fl oz soured cream
3 tbsps white wine vinegar
Pinch salt
200g/7oz Mascarpone
2 tbsps milk
2 tbsps chopped chives
Pinch celery salt
200g/7oz cooked ham (in slices without rind)
400g/14oz canned palm hearts

Preparation time:
0 minutes
Cooking time:
0 minutes
Nutritional value:
analysis per serving, approx:
1890kJ/450kcal
23g protein
23g fat
39g carbohydrate

Peel the onion and chop. Fry in oil until soft. Mix together the curry powder and rice, add to the onions and fry for a few minutes before adding the chicken stock. Cover and cook over a gentle heat for 20 minutes. • Rinse and trim the pepper, then dry and dice. Peel the banana and pineapple and slice thinly. • Leave the rice to cool. Carefully stir in the pepper, banana, mango chutney, soured cream, vinegar and salt. • Blend the milk and Mascarpone. Sprinkle with the celery salt and add the chopped chives. Spread the mixture on the ham slices, followed by the drained palm hearts. Roll the ham loosely and then cut diagonally. Arrange the slices around the rice salad.

Wholewheat Pasta Salad

250g/8oz lean minced steak
1 egg
1 tbsp oat flakes
1 tbsp currants
2 tbsps desiccated coconut
1 tsp curry powder
1 tsp chopped basil leaves
1½ tsps salt
3 tbsps sunflower oil
150g/½oz wholewheat pasta twists
2 bananas
100g/4oz young spinach
2 tbsps roast, salted peanuts
3 tbsps sour cream
1 tsp mustard
1 tsp honey
Pinch of freshly ground white pepper
Juice ½ lemon

Preparation time:
45 minutes
Nutritional value:
Analysis per serving, approx:
• 1680kJ/400kcal
• 24g protein
• 18g fat
• 36g carbohydrate

Mix the minced steak thoroughly with the egg, oat flakes, the rinsed and drained currants, half a tablespoon of desiccated coconut, half a teaspoon of curry powder, basil leaves and half a teaspoon of salt. Shape into balls about the size of walnuts, roll in the remaining desiccated coconut and fry in 2 tablespoons of oil for 10 minutes or until crisp and brown. • Cook the pasta for 10 minutes in 1½l/2¾ pints water. Leave to drain. • Peel the bananas. Cut one banana into thin slices. Rinse the spinach, discard any yellowed leaves and drain well. Cut the leaves into thin strips. Fill a bowl with the pasta twists, meatballs, banana slices and peanuts. • Break the other banana into chunks and mix with the soured cream, mustard, honey, the remaining curry powder, a pinch of salt, pepper, lemon juice and the remaining oil. Purée the mixture in a blender, add the spinach strips and combine with the pasta and meatballs.

Pasta Salad with Vegetables

125g/5oz pasta shells or bows
2l/3½ pints water
2 tsps salt
250g/8oz peas in their pods
6 spring onions
250g/8oz small tomatoes
250g/8oz cucumber
150g/5½oz German pork sausage (unsliced)
Bunch dill
1 small garlic clove
3 tbsps vinegar
½ tsp hot paprika or chilli sauce
2 tbsps corn oil

Preparation time:
30 minutes
Marinating time:
30 minutes
Nutritional value:
Analysis per serving, approx:
  1510kJ/360kcal
  13g protein
  17g fat
  36g carbohydrate

To cook the pasta, bring the water and a teaspoon of salt to the boil. Add the pasta and cook for 8-10 minutes until al dente. Drain and leave to cool. • Shell the peas, rinse and cook in salted water for 5 minutes. Drain. Rinse and trim the spring onions and chop into rings. Rinse the tomatoes, dry, halve, remove the stalks and quarter. Rinse the cucumber, halve lengthways and cut into thin slices. Cut the sausage into strips and chop the dill leaves finely. Mix all the prepared ingredients together in a bowl. • To prepare the sauce, peel and chop the garlic clove and mix with the vinegar, a pinch of salt, paprika or chilli sauce and oil. • Combine the pasta and vegetables with the sauce and leave to marinate for 30 minutes before serving.

Vitello Tonnato

500g/1lb 2oz leg of veal
Bunch mixed herbs
1 clove garlic
1 bay leaf
1 tsp salt
1l/1¾ pints chicken stock
250ml/8fl oz dry white wine
Bunch parsley
1 egg yolk
4 anchovy fillets
210g/7oz can of tuna (in brine)
3 tbsps capers
2 tbsps corn oil
100ml/3fl oz whipping cream
1 lemon
Pinch of freshly ground white pepper

Rinse the meat. Rinse and trim the mixed herbs, then chop them coarsely. Peel the garlic clove. Boil the chicken stock and add the veal herbs, bay leaf and garlic. Simmer for 1½ hours. • Add the white wine and rinsed parsley. Leave to cool for at least 6 hours. •To prepare the sauce, purée the egg yolk, anchovy fillets, drained tuna and 2 tablespoons of capers. Stir in the oil slowly. Add 5 tablespoons of the veal stock, partially-whipped cream and the juice of half a lemon. Season with pepper. • Slice the veal thinly. Fold the slices and pour over the sauce. Garnish with slices of lemon and the remaining capers.

Preparation time:
2 hours
Standing time:
6 hours
Nutritional value:
Analysis per serving, approx:
• 1890kJ/450kcal
• 44g protein
• 24g fat
• 3g carbohydrate

Meat Puffs

To make 9 puffs:
300g/10oz frozen puff pastry
2 spring onions
100g/4oz button mushrooms
2 tbsps sesame oil
250g/8oz minced pork
1 tsp Chinese five-spice powder
50g/2oz bean sprouts (canned)
2 tbsps soya sauce
1 egg
2 tbsps sesame seeds

Thawing time:
30 minutes
Preparation time:
35 minutes
Baking time:
25 minutes
Nutritional value:
Analysis per puff, approx:
• 1090kJ/260kcal
• 9g protein
• 19g fat
• 12g carbohydrate

Leave the puff pastry to thaw at room temperature. Rinse, dry and trim the spring onions. Cut the white onion stalk into rings. Rinse the mushrooms and chop. • Heat the oil and fry the minced pork for 3 minutes, breaking up any lumps with a fork. Add the onions, mushrooms and Chinese five-spice powder. Cook for another 5 minutes, stirring frequently. Rinse and drain the bean sprouts. Add to the minced pork together with the soya sauce. Cook for a further 2 minutes. Leave to cool. • Heat the oven to 210°C/415°F/gas mark 6-7. Rinse a baking tray in cold water. • Roll out the dough on a floured work top into a sheet about 35cm/14 inches square. Cut it into nine small squares. Brush each one with water. Spoon some of the filling onto one half of the square and fold over, pressing down firmly at the edges. Whisk the egg. Brush the top of each puff with the egg and sprinkle with sesame seeds. • Place the puffs on the moist baking tray and bake in the middle of the oven for about 25 minutes, or until golden.

Crostini

To make 16:
150g/5½oz chicken livers
1 onion
30g/1oz butter
2 tbsps Marsala
1 tbsp capers
Salt and freshly ground black pepper
100g/4oz black olives
1 onion
1 garlic clove
2 anchovy fillets
1 tbsp capers
5 tbsps olive oil
1 tbsp chopped parsley
Pinch sugar
200g/7oz French stick

Preparation time:
1 hour
Nutritional value:
Analysis per serving, approx:
• 460kJ/110kcal per slice
• 4g protein
• 7g fat
• 8g carbohydrate

To prepare the paste, rinse the chicken livers and pat dry. Peel and chop the onion. Heat the butter in a frying pan and fry the onion until golden brown. Add the livers and brown lightly on both sides. Remove and chop finely. Pour the Marsala into the butter and liver juices, stir well, then mix in the chopped livers. Chop the capers and add them to the livers together with some salt and pepper. • To prepare the olive paste, stone the olives and chop well. Peel and chop the onion. Crush the garlic clove, anchovy fillets and capers using a pestle and mortar, then add this mixture to the onions and olives. Mix in the chopped parsley and 1 tablespoon of olive oil. Season with pepper and sugar. • Cut the bread into 16 equal slices. Heat the remaining olive oil in a frying pan and fry the slices on both sides until brown and crisp. • Spread 8 slices with the liver paste and 8 slices with the olive paste. • Serve the crostini warm.

Rye-grain Balls with Ham

To make 25:
100g/4oz raw ham
100g/4oz finely ground rye grains
Salt and black pepper
½ tsp paprika
½ tsp dried thyme
½ tsp ground coriander
½ tsp ground caraway seed
3 tbsps chopped chives
50g/2oz grated Emmental cheese
2 eggs
3 tbsps olive oil
3 tsps coriander seed
3 tbsps caraway seed

Preparation time:
25 minutes

Frying time:
10-15 minutes
Nutritional value:
Analysis per ball, approx:
• 210kJ/50kcal
• 2g protein
• 3g fat
• 3g carbohydrate

Chop the ham finely and mix together with the rye grains, spices, chives and the cheese. • Whisk the eggs with 2 tablespoons of oil and 1 to 2 tablespoons of water. Combine with the ham mixture. Leave to stand for 10 minutes, then shape the 'dough' into small balls and dip them in the seeds • Shallow-fry the balls in the rest of the oil until crisp.

Grain Balls with Mushrooms

To make 25:
200g/7oz button mushrooms
Juice ½ lemon
1 onion
100g/4oz finely ground cracked wheat
2 tbsps finely chopped parsley
2 eggs
4 tbsps sunflower oil
4 tbsps wholewheat breadcrumbs
3 tbsps sesame seeds

2 tsps vegetable stock granules
Freshly ground black pepper

Preparation time:
20 minutes
Frying time:
10-15 minutes
Nutritional value:
Analysis per ball, approx:
• 180kJ/45kcal
• 2g protein
• 2g fat
• 4g carbohydrate

Rinse the mushrooms and chop finely. Sprinkle with lemon juice. Peel and chop the onion. Mix the cracked wheat with the stock granules, pepper and 4 tablespoons of boiling water. Add the mushrooms, parsley and onion and then stir in the eggs, 2 tablespoons of oil and bread–crumbs. Leave the 'dough' to stand for 10 minutes, then shape it into balls. Dip them in the sesame seeds and fry in oil until crisp.

Wheat-grain Balls with Walnuts

To make 25:
100g/4oz finely ground wheat
100g/4oz ground walnuts
100g/4oz coarsely grated Gouda cheese
salt and white pepper
1 tsp paprika
1 tsp chopped basil
2 tbsps chopped parsley
2 eggs
2 tbsps sesame oil
3 tbsps poppyseeds

Nutritional value:
Analysis per ball, approx:
• 315kJ/75kcal
• 2g protein
• 6g fat
• 3g carbohydrate

Mix the grains with the walnuts, cheese, herbs and spices. Whisk the eggs with 2 tablespoons of water and stir into the grain and nut mixture. Leave to stand for 10 minutes. • Shape the 'dough' into balls, dip them in the poppyseeds and fry in oil.

Preparation time:
minutes
Frying time:
–15 minutes

Grilled Avocados

2 avocados (about 400g/14oz)
2 tsps lemon juice
12 anchovy fillets
2 tbsps small capers
½ onion
Dash of Tabasco sauce
1 tbsp walnut oil
4 tbsps crème fraîche
2 slices Cheddar cheese

Preparation time:
10 minutes
Cooking time:
10-15 minutes
Nutritional value:
Analysis per serving, approx:
• 1365kJ/325kcal
• 7g protein
• 30g fat
• 6g carbohydrate

Preheat the oven to 230°C/450°F/Gas Mark 8, or turn on the electric grill.• Wash, dry and halve the avocados and remove the stones. Remove two-thirds of the flesh, chop finely, and drizzle lemon juice over both the flesh remaining in the skin and the chopped avocado.• Cut a sliver off the rounded bottom of the halved avocado so that they sit firmly. Chop the anchovies, capers and peeled half-onion finely, and combine with the chopped avocado, Tabasco sauce, oil and crème fraîche. Stuff the avocados with the creamy mixture, and place on the a baking dish in the oven or under the grill. Dice the slices of cheese and scatter over the avocados.•Bake or grill until the cheese has melted and a golden-brown crust has formed.

Our Tip: For the filling, 2 chopped herring fillets and a gherkin may be substituted for the anchovies and capers.

Fennel with Aïoli

medium-sized fennel bulbs
(about 800g/1¾lbs)
tsps lemon juice
egg-sized piece of white
crustless bread
cup milk
cloves garlic
egg yolks
250ml/8fl oz cold-pressed
olive oil
-2 tsps tarragon vinegar
tsp salt
pinch of white pepper

Preparation time:
0 minutes

Nutritional value:
analysis per serving, approx:
about 3130kJ/745kcal
8g protein
7g fat
7g carbohydrate

Remove the feathery green leaves from the fennel bulbs, wash and pat dry. Chop finely, cover, and set aside.•

Discard the outer tough ribs of the fennel bulbs. Shred the fennel, sprinkle with the lemon juice, cover and set aside.• Soak the bread in the cold milk. Peel the garlic and crush through a garlic press into a bowl. Squeeze any excess moisture from the moistened bread, add it and the egg yolks to the crushed garlic, and mix well. Then add the olive oil into the garlic mixture, a drop at a time to start with, then a teaspoonful at a time until you have a sauce with the consistency of mayonnaise. Flavour to taste with the tarragon vinegar, salt and pepper. Serve the aïoli in a small bowl sprinkled with the chopped fennel green. • Place the bowl on a tray with the fennel arranged around it. The strips of fennel are eaten with the aïoli sauce.• Fresh French bread and dry white wine are good accompaniments.

Pumpernickel with Mascarpone

4 slices pumpernickel bread
(180g/6oz)
1 punnet cress
75g/3oz lean raw ham
200g/7oz mascarpone
Pinch cayenne
4 small peach halves (canned)

Preparation time:
20 minutes
Nutritional value:
Analysis per serving, approx:
• 1590kJ/380kcal
• 11g protein
• 23g fat
• 30g carbohydrate

Cut each pumpernickel slice into three equal fingers. Cut off the cress with a pair of scissors and rinse in cold water. Take two-thirds of the cress and chop finely. Cut the ham into small squares. • Mix the mascarpone with the chopped cress, the ham squares and a little juice from the canned peaches. Season the mixture with cayenne and spread on the pumpernickel slices. Chop each peach half into six wedges and arrange two pieces on each pumpernickel finger. Finally garnish with the remaining cress.

Toasted Wholemeal Bread with Bacon

8 slices thick-cut wholemeal
bread
8 thin rashers rindless bacon
(75g/3oz)
3 tomatoes
4 iceberg lettuce leaves
2 tbsps Remoulade sauce

Preparation time:
20 minutes
Nutritional value:
Analysis per serving, approx:
• 1380kJ/330kcal
• 7g protein
• 21g fat
• 29g carbohydrate

Toast the bread. • Fry the bacon in a frying pan without fat until crisp, then halve the rashers. Rinse the tomatoes, pat dry, remove the stalk and cut into slices. Rinse and dry the lettuce leaves and cut into quarters. • Coat the toasted bread with the Remoulade sauce. Arrange the tomato slices on top and then cut each sandwich in half diagonally. Place one piece of ham on each triangle and garnish with lettuce leaves.

Rye Bread with Creamed Avocado

225g/5oz prawns
4 slices rye bread (200g/7oz)
50g/2oz butter
1 small onion
½ red pepper
some dill leaves
1 tbsp lemon juice
1 ripe avocado
½ tsp salt
freshly ground black pepper

Preparation time:
30 minutes
Nutritional value:
analysis per serving, approx:
1590kJ/380kcal
10g protein
26g fat
26g carbohydrate

Rinse and drain the prawns, then cut into small pieces. • Butter the bread and cut each slice into three equal fingers. • Peel the onion, rinse the red pepper and cut both into cubes. Rinse the dill, spin dry and chop coarsely. Mix the onion, red pepper, dill and prawns with the lemon juice. • Peel and purée the avocado and stir in the prawn mixture. Season with salt and pepper and spread on the rye bread fingers.

Wholewheat Crackers

To make 40:
For the dough:
300g/10oz wholemeal flour
50g/2oz wholemeal barley
flour
2 tsps baking powder
1 tsp salt
Pinch white pepper
Pinch freshly grated nutmeg
150g/5½oz natural yogurt
150g/5½oz margarine
1 egg
2 tbsps sesame seeds
For the topping:
150g/5½oz margarine
150g/5½oz mascarpone
250g/8oz cottage cheese
1 tsp salt
1 tsp sweet paprika
1 tsp pink peppercorns
1 tsp tomato purée
1 tsp curry powder
Generous pinch turmeric
1 small grated onion
1 ripe avocado
1 tsp green peppercorns
Pinch black pepper

Preparation time:
1 hour
Baking time:
15 minutes
Nutritional value:
Analysis per cracker, approx:
• 505kJ/120kcal
• 3g protein
• 9g fat
• 7g carbohydrate

Make a smooth dough from the wheat and barley flour, baking powder, spices, yogurt and margarine and leave it to rest in a cool place for 15 minutes. • Heat the oven to 180°C/350°F/ gas mark 4. • Roll out the dough to a thickness of 3mm/¼ inch. Cut out the crackers and place them on a greased baking tray. Brush on a little beaten egg and then sprinkle a few sesame seeds on top. Bake for about 15 minutes. • Beat the margarine with the Mascarpone, cottage cheese and salt until creamy. Divide into four parts. Mix one part with the paprika, crushed pink peppercorns and tomato purée the second with the curry

owder, turmeric and onion,
e third with puréed avocado
sh and crushed green
ppers and the last with black
pper. • Pipe the cream on to
e crackers and decorate with
ppings.

Avocado Wedges

To make 8:
2 ripe avocados
2 tbsps lemon juice
Salt and garlic pepper
125g/5oz Edam cheese
8 slices cured pork
½ punnet cress

Preparation time:
10 minutes
Nutritional value:
Analysis per wedge, approx:
• 970kJ/230kcal
• 7g protein
• 21g fat
• 2g carbohydrate

Quarter the avocados and remove the stone. Peel the fruit and sprinkle with lemon juice to prevent discolouration. Shake salt and garlic pepper over the avocado. If serving as an hors d'oeuvre,

allow two wedges per portion.
• Cut the rind off the Edam cheese and make eight cubes. Remove the rind from the pork slices. Secure the folded pork to the avocado wedge with a cocktail stick surmounted with a cube of cheese. • Snip and rinse the cress, then arrange bundles under the ham.

Our tip: When buying avocados take care that the fruit is really ripe. The flesh should yield when light pressure is applied. Unripe avocados should be stored for a few days at room temperature. If you are unable to find any garlic pepper, then rub the avocado flesh with a cut garlic clove and sprinkle with a little freshly ground pepper. In this way, only a hint of garlic will be detected.

Aubergines with Feta Cheese

4 aubergines
1 tsp salt
10 tbsps olive oil
2 garlic cloves
Freshly ground white pepper
Juice 1 lemon
Sprig fresh thyme or 2 tsps
dried thyme
4 small tomatoes
200g/7oz Feta cheese

Preparation time:
10 minutes
Marinating time:
2–3 hours
Nutritional value:
Analysis per serving, approx:
1090kJ/260kcal
12g protein
19g fat
12g carbohydrate

R inse the aubergines, pat
them dry and trim the
stalks. Cut them into slices,
sprinkle with salt and leave to
stand for 10 minutes. • Dry the
aubergine slices and brown
them on both sides in a large
frying pan. Set aside. Peel and
crush the garlic cloves, then fry
them in the oil until golden
brown. Brush the garlic and oil
on the aubergine slices,
sprinkle with a little pepper
and some lemon juice. • If
using fresh thyme leaves, rinse
and shake them dry. Scatter
fresh thyme leaves (or the
crushed dried leaves) over the
aubergine slices. Layer the
aubergine slices in a bowl and
leave them to stand for 2–3
hours. • Rinse the tomatoes,
remove the stalks and arrange
alternate slices of tomato and
Feta cheese in a dish. Arrange
the aubergines alongside. •
Serve with French bread.

Tofu and Vegetable Salad

300g/10oz tofu
2 tbsps soya sauce
2 tbsps cider vinegar
2 tbsps soya oil
Freshly ground black pepper
500g/1lb 2oz tomatoes
250g/8oz green peppers
250g/8oz cucumber
2 small onions
2 tbsps sesame seeds

Preparation time:
45 minutes
Nutritional value:
Analysis per serving, approx:
• 880kJ/210kcal
• 10g protein
• 11g fat
• 16g carbohydrate

Cut the tofu into 1cm/½-inch cubes. Place in a bowl with the soy sauce, vinegar and half a tablespoon of oil. Sprinkle with pepper and stir well. Leave the tofu to marinate for about 10 minutes, stirring occasionally. • Score the tomatoes with a sharp knife, immerse in boiling hot water for a few seconds and remove the skin. Discard the stalk, seeds and liquid, before cutting into segments. Quarter the green peppers and discard the stalks, seeds and pith. Blanch in boiling water for a few seconds, then plunge immediately into cold water. Slice across the peppers to make thin strips. Peel the cucumber, rinse and cut into 1cm/½-inch cubes. Peel the onions and slice thinly. •Place all the prepared ingredients in a bowl and pour on the tofu marinade. • Mix the sesame seeds with the tofu cubes. Heat the rest of the oil in a frying pan and fry the cubes for about 10 minutes over a medium heat, stirring frequently. Mix with the vegetables, allow to cool and serve.

Mushrooms à la Grecque

200g/7oz shallots
2 cloves garlic
400g/14oz button mushrooms
2 tbsps olive oil
1 tsp fennel seeds
1 tsp coriander seeds
½ tsp salt
125ml/4fl oz dry white wine
½ tsp freshly chopped basil
Juice ½ lemon
Freshly ground white pepper
(optional)

Preparation time:
20 minutes
Chilling time:
1 hour
Nutritional value:
Analysis per serving, approx:
• 420kJ/100kcal
• 2g protein
• 4g fat
• 7g carbohydrate

Peel the garlic and shallots. Halve or quarter any large shallots and chop the garlic finely. Rinse and trim the mushrooms. Pat dry, halving any larger ones. • Heat the oil in a large frying pan. Fry the shallots and garlic over a gentle heat until soft. • Crush the fennel and coriander seeds coarsely using a pestle and mortar. Add to the onions together with the mushrooms. Sprinkle with salt and cook for 5 minutes over a gentle heat, stirring frequently. • Add the wine and basil and cook for a further 5 minutes. • Remove the pan from the heat and add the lemon juice. Season the mushrooms with pepper, if required. • Chill the mushrooms and serve in small portions. • Serve with crisply toasted rye or wholemeal bread.

Artichokes with Herb Mayonnaise

4 artichokes
1l/1¾ pints water
2 tsps salt
1 tbsp lemon juice
For the herb mayonnaise:
2 small egg yolks
Salt and freshly ground white pepper
Pinch sugar
1 tsp mustard
1 tsp lemon juice
125ml/4fl oz corn oil
1 tsp vinegar
Bunch of mixed herbs, such as chervil, chives, dill, thyme and tarragon

Preparation time:
5 minutes
Nutritional value:
Analysis per serving, approx:
1220kJ/290kcal
6g protein
19g fat
2g carbohydrate

Cut off the stem and hard, outer leaves of the artichoke. Use kitchen scissors to trim off the tops of the leaves, reducing them by about a third. • Bring the water, salt and lemon juice to the boil. Rinse the artichokes and cook for 40 minutes with the stalks downwards. • Beat the egg yolks with the salt, sugar, pepper and mustard. Add the lemon juice. Add the oil to the egg yolks a drop at a time, whisking constantly, then increase to a trickle until it has all been added. If the mayonnaise becomes too thick, add a few drops of vinegar. Rinse the herbs, pat dry, chop finely and then mix into the mayonnaise. • Serve the herb mayonnaise with the drained artichokes.

Our tip: *To eat artichokes, tear off one leaf at a time and dip the end in the mayonnaise. Eat only the artichoke flesh and mayonnaise, discarding the tough outer leaf.*

Avocado Salad

2 avocados
1 red pepper
1 stick celery
½ onion
4 gherkins
100g/4oz low-fat curd cheese
1 egg yolk
2 tbsps corn oil
1 tbsp lemon juice
1 tsp mustard
Dash of Worcestershire sauce
1 tsp salt
¼ tsp white pepper
2 tbsps small capers, rinsed and drained

Preparation time:
10 minutes
Nutritional value:
Analysis per serving, approx:
• 1220kJ/290kcal
• 7g protein
• 25g fat
• 9g carbohydrate

Quarter the avocados. Remove the stones, peel, and cut into thin slices. Halve the pepper, remove the pith and seeds; wash, dry and chop the pepper halves. Wash the celery and cut into thin slices. Peel and dice the onion. Chop the gherkins. • Mix the curd cheese with the egg yolk, oil, lemon juice, mustard, Worcestershire sauce, salt, pepper and capers. • Mix the sliced avocado, diced pepper, sliced celery, diced onion and gherkins with the dressing.

Our Tip: *This recipe requires forward planning. The avocados must be completely ripe. Only fully ripe fruit have the characteristic, subtle avocado taste. Unripe avocados will ripen if kept in a paper bag and left in an airing cupboard for 2-3 days.*

Classic Cheese Soufflé

75g/3oz butter
75g/3oz flour
375ml/14fl oz warm milk
Pinch freshly grated nutmeg
2 pinches cayenne
5 eggs
125g/5oz Emmental cheese
For the dish:
15g/½oz butter for greasing
1 tbsp freshly grated Parmesan cheese
½ tsp flour

Preparation time:
40 minutes
Baking time:
25-30 minutes
Nutritional value:
Analysis per serving, approx:
• 2010kJ/480kcal
• 21g protein
• 36g fat
• 16g carbohydrate

Smear the inside of a soufflé dish with the butter for greasing. Mix the flour and Parmesan cheese and sprinkle i carefully onto the butter. Heat the oven to 200°C/400°F/gas mark 6. • Melt the butter for the soufflé base in a saucepan, but do not brown. Stir in the flour and cook gently, slowly adding the milk. Whisk constantly. Bring the thickene milk to the boil and remove from the heat. Season with th nutmeg and cayenne. • Separate the eggs and add the egg yolks to the hot sauce on at a time. Grate the cheese an stir into the sauce. Whisk the egg whites until stiff. Fold the egg whites into the cooled sauce without stirring. • Pour the whisked soufflé mix into the dish and then bake for 25 30 minutes. Do not open the oven during the cooking tim • Serve the soufflé at once wi a green salad.

Pea Soufflé

300g/10oz garden peas
1½ tsps salt
100g/4oz Emmental cheese
5 eggs
Pinch grated nutmeg
Pinch cayenne
1 tbsps medium sherry
250g/8oz cooked ham cut into
slices (without rind)
1 onion
25g/½oz butter
Bunch chervil
100g/4oz crème fraîche
Oil for greasing the ramekins
(10cm/4 inches diameter)

Preparation time:
30 minutes
Baking time:
25 minutes
Nutritional value:
Analysis per serving, approx:
2180kJ/520kcal
33g protein
38g fat
14g carbohydrate

Boil the peas with half a teaspoon of salt for 10 minutes. Grate the cheese. Separate two eggs. Mix the cheese with the egg yolks, nutmeg, cayenne and sherry. Lay the ham slices in a line so that they overlap. Coat with the mixture and shape into a long roll. Cut the roll into 3cm/1-inch slices. • Drain the peas and leave to cool. Peel and chop the onion and fry in butter until golden. Rinse the chervil, shake dry and snip off any thick stalks. • Heat the oven to 200°C/400°F/gas mark 6. Grease the ramekins. •Purée the peas with the chopped onion, chervil and crème fraîche in a blender. Slowly add the remaining 3 eggs, the egg whites and the rest of the salt. Spoon the purée into the ramekins and arrange the ham and cheese rolls upright on top. • Bake the soufflés on the middle shelf of the oven for about 25 minutes.

Index